Reviving Play
The Importance of Playfulness for Adult Mental Health

Table of Contents

1. Introduction 1
2. Understanding Play: A Lifelong Necessity 2
   - 2.1. The Mechanics of Play: Neurological and Psychological Perspectives 2
   - 2.2. Play in Childhood: Building Blocks of Personality 3
   - 2.3. Adolescent Play: Transitioning Roles and Responsibilities 3
   - 2.4. Adulthood: Where Playfulness Recedes 4
   - 2.5. Play in the Golden Years: Promoting Longevity and Mental Agility 4
3. Rediscovering Joy: The Psychological Benefits of Playfulness 6
   - 3.1. Theoretical Framing of Playfulness 6
   - 3.2. The Concept of Adult Playfulness 6
   - 3.3. The Psychological Aspects of Playfulness 7
   - 3.4. Creativity and Innovation Through Play 7
   - 3.5. Social Connectivity Through Play 8
   - 3.6. Stress Management and Playfulness 8
   - 3.7. Playfulness and Productivity 8
   - 3.8. Cultivating a Playful Attitude 9
4. Stress-Busting: How Play Alleviates Adult Anxieties 10
   - 4.1. The Science of Stress and Play 10
   - 4.2. Forms of Adult Play 10
     - 4.2.1. Indoor and Outdoor Play 11
     - 4.2.2. Digital Play 11
   - 4.3. The Power of Laughter 11
   - 4.4. Play and Social Connections 11
   - 4.5. Nurturing Mindfulness through Play 12
   - 4.6. Play as a Form of Exercise 12
   - 4.7. Circumventing Adult Barriers to Play 12

5. From Recess to the Office: Injecting Play into Everyday Life 14
   5.1. Why Bring Play to Work? 14
   5.2. Practical Strategies to Inject Play 15
   5.3. The Diverse Faces of Play 15
   5.4. Transforming Stress into Playfulness 16
   5.5. Conclusion 17
6. Bonding Over Laughter: The Social Dynamics of Play 18
   6.1. The Science Behind Bonding and Laughter 18
   6.2. Play Leads to Laughter 19
   6.3. Shared Laughter as a Social Glue 19
   6.4. Laughter in the Workplace 19
   6.5. Boosting Morale Through Laughter 20
   6.6. Play and Laughter in a Digital World 20
   6.7. Concluding Notes 21
7. Boosting Creativity: The Link between Playfulness and Innovation 22
   7.1. The Nature of Playfulness and Creativity: A Primordial Connection 22
   7.2. Exploring Psychological Underpinnings 22
   7.3. A Biopsychological View 23
   7.4. Case Studies: From Silicon Valley to Scandinavian Schools .. 23
   7.5. Practical Ways to Boost Creativity through Play 24
   7.6. Conclusion: Playfulness – The Gateway to Innovation 24
8. Overcoming Barriers: Shedding the Taboos Around Adult Play .. 26
   8.1. Unlearning Societal Expectations 26
   8.2. Overcoming Fear of Judgment 26
   8.3. Reevaluating the Perception of Time 27
   8.4. Shifting Away from Excessive Digitization 27
   8.5. Reconnecting with the Joy of Play 28
9. Play as Therapy: Case Studies of Success 29

- 9.1. The Case of John: Small Changes, Big Impact ... 29
- 9.2. Sandra's Story: Play Enhancing Communication ... 30
- 9.3. Adam's Experience: Transformative Role-playing ... 30
- 10. Guided Games: Practical Approaches to Adult Playfulness ... 32
  - 10.1. Reclaiming Play as Adults ... 32
  - 10.2. Games as Vehicles of Play ... 32
  - 10.3. Creating a Game Plan ... 33
  - 10.4. Embracing Solo Play ... 33
  - 10.5. Facilitating Social Connection Through Games ... 33
  - 10.6. Virtual Games: Gateway to a Digital Playground ... 34
  - 10.7. The Therapeutic Power of Role-Playing Games ... 34
  - 10.8. Balancing Play and Responsibility ... 34
- 11. Stepping into the Future: The Evolution of Play for Enhanced Well-being ... 36
  - 11.1. The Play in Prehistory ... 36
  - 11.2. Moving to Agricultural and Industrial Eras ... 36
  - 11.3. Post-Industrial Age and the Rise of Structured Leisure ... 37
  - 11.4. The Digital Age: Play and Technology ... 37
  - 11.5. Futuristic Visions: Play for Wellness ... 37
  - 11.6. Play Therapy: Healing through Play ... 38
  - 11.7. Gamification: Combining Work and Play ... 38
  - 11.8. Play-Based Interventions for Wellness ... 38
  - 11.9. Embracing Playfulness: A Journey towards Wholeness ... 39

Chapter 1. Introduction

In the hustle and bustle of an often stressful contemporary life, the purity and joy of playfulness can become a forgotten relic from childhood. However, this riveting Special Report, titled 'Reviving Play: The Importance of Playfulness for Adult Mental Health', aims to change this perceptual gap. With a refreshing blend of scientific evidence, expert testimonies, and practical, straight-forward guidelines, we delve into the exhilarating world where grown-up responsibilities coexist beautifully with child-like playfulness. Discover how reintroducing fun and games into your daily routine can provide significant benefits for mental health, efficiency, and overall happiness. Not only does this report promise a fascinating read, it invites you on a journey to reignite your personal spark and look at life through a fresher, more vibrant lens. Awaken your cognitive curiosity and boost your sense of well-being, because playing isn't just for children anymore!

Chapter 2. Understanding Play: A Lifelong Necessity

Play, most often associated with childhood, is a term loaded with myriad implications, despite its lighthearted inference of fun-filled activities. From a psychological perspective, it represents a critical cornerstone across a spectrum of cognitive and emotional development. Those who consciously evoke playfulness throughout their lives tend to maintain better mental agility, emotional robustness, and social capability. But how does play work its magic, and why is it a lifelong necessity?

2.1. The Mechanics of Play: Neurological and Psychological Perspectives

Unravelling the mystery of play starts from understanding its biological footprint. Neuroscientists, eager to glean insights about the potent effects of play, have turned their gaze towards our brain's inner workings during playtime. Under the microscope, you will observe a fascinating dance of neurochemical escapades that reinforce our propensity towards play.

When we engage in playful activities, the brain releases "feel good" neurotransmitters including dopamine, serotonin and endorphins. Dopamine is associated with the brain's reward system, improving mood, motivation and attention. Serotonin promotes feelings of well-being and security, while endorphins act as natural painkillers, eliciting feelings similar to that of morphine.

Apart from the neurochemical spikes, play also stimulates the growth of new neurons and helps build the architecture of the developing brain. It enhances cognitive functions—boosting creativity, problem-solving abilities, and improving adaptability to novel situations.

2.2. Play in Childhood: Building Blocks of Personality

Contrary to popular perception, play during childhood isn't just mindless fun; each giggle, every playful chase carries profound implications. Through play, children gradually navigate the complexities of their physical world, developing coordination and strength. They enact adult roles, providing a basis for understanding social norms and cultural practices.

In a broader psychological context, play fosters self-discovery, bolsters self-confidence, and nurtures emotional resilience. Swiss psychologist Jean Piaget, famous for his studies on children, emphasized play as the essence of childhood cognitive development. Play, to Piaget, was the window through which children gain an understanding of their world.

2.3. Adolescent Play: Transitioning Roles and Responsibilities

The significance of play doesn't fade away as children grow into teenagers. It evolves, fostering skills associated with adult roles and responsibilities. Play becomes a protective factor, a buffer against the external pressures of adolescence. Simultaneously, it contributes to the development of a range of socio-cognitive skills, enabling adolescents to transition with greater ease into adulthood.

During adolescence, play begins to revolve around peer interactions, team-building activities, competition, and complex strategies. It continues to serve as a learning mechanism, shaping their social aptitude, emotional maturity, and identity.

2.4. Adulthood: Where Playfulness Recedes

As individuals transition into adulthood, play is often relegated to the periphery. Overwhelmed by obligations and responsibilities, adults erroneously dismiss play as unproductive and frivolous. However, this cultural perception robs adults of a significant tool for maintaining mental health and cognitive agility.

Play in adulthood takes varied forms, from engaging in creative endeavors and intellectual challenges to nurturing a playful attitude in the everyday tasks at hand. When adults engage in play, they are essentially flexing their cognitive muscles, exploring their creativity, and nurturing their emotional health. The underlying rewards of play—reduced stress, fortified relationships, improved cognitive functions, increased productivity—are an antidote to many adult stresses and tribulations.

2.5. Play in the Golden Years: Promoting Longevity and Mental Agility

In the golden years, the importance of play persists. It promotes emotional well-being, reduces risk of cognitive decline, and can improve physical health. Fostering a spirit of playfulness can not only contribute to quality of life but also promote longevity.

Evolving research shows that play can stave off dementia, maintain social connections, and help elders adapt to the physical and emotional challenges of ageing. Even simple forms of play like puzzles, gardening, painting, or storytelling can aid in maintaining mental and physical vitality and independence.

In essence, play is a lifelong necessity and not just a pursuit of leisure. From shaping the cornerstone of early developmental stages to aiding in the transition towards adulthood and then to maintaining cognitive, emotional, and social health during the later stages of life, play continues to remain a potent tool. It pays to remember that joy, laughter, and curiosity - the spirits of playfulness - do not come with an expiration date. They are the essential ingredients in the recipe of a vibrant, healthy life. Hence, play should not only be reserved for children. Indeed, it should be woven into the very fabric of human existence, from the beginning till the end.

Chapter 3. Rediscovering Joy: The Psychological Benefits of Playfulness

Drawing from the poetic resonance of Mary Oliver's poignant query, "What will you do with your one wild and precious life?", let's start this expedition by consciously choosing to infuse it with an element of playfulness.

3.1. Theoretical Framing of Playfulness

Playfulness, the act of engaging in light-hearted and fun activities, has long been the subject of study for its tremendous benefits. Jean Piaget, the Swiss psychologist, best remembered for his work on child development, emphasized its vital role in the cognitive and social development of children. However, it is important to note the relevance of playfulness extends beyond the early phases of life. Researchers like Dr. Stuart Brown have proven that the attributes of playfulness bear significant influence in adult life by fostering creativity, enhancing problem-solving skills, and generating deep emotional connections with others. Our exploration is grounded in this framework that understands playfulness as a potent force contributing to adult mental well-being.

3.2. The Concept of Adult Playfulness

Adult playfulness often gets bypassed amidst the myriad responsibilities and commitments of the grown-up world. However, it bears holistic transformative potential. Playfulness covers a wide range of activities that induce joy, laughter, and a sense of lightheartedness. It is about making a deliberate choice to tap into the free-spiritedness of our internal child. Studies reveal feelings of exhilaration, liberation, and creativity accompanying such deliberate playful activities. Dr. Anthony DeBenedet states in his book 'Playful Intelligence' that, "Play is the ultimate vulnerability – it's where we explore, experiment, and push boundaries."

3.3. The Psychological Aspects of Playfulness

A psychological exploration of playfulness shows promising advantages. Play has a direct correlation to the release of endorphins, chemicals in the brain that act as natural stress-relievers and mood-enhancers. Moreover, it also stimulates the brain's production of dopamine, which promotes feelings of pleasure and satisfaction. Research also establishes that playful activities can help manage anxiety and depression, two prevalent mental health concerns in today's world.

3.4. Creativity and Innovation Through Play

Creativity and innovation have a symbiotic relationship with playfulness. Playing exposes us to a different range of perspectives, allowing us to think in non-linear ways, encouraging spontaneity, and enabling explorative thinking. This fosters an environment conducive to innovation, helping both individuals and organizations thrive. Google's '80/20 Time', which allowed engineers to spend 80% of their time on core projects and 20% on activities they are passionate about, highlights how fostering playfulness promotes creative problem solving, leading to inventions like Gmail and AdSense.

3.5. Social Connectivity Through Play

Playfulness also powerfully influences social dynamics. Play fosters camaraderie and understanding among individuals, creating bridges of empathy and helping to form deeper emotional ties. Whether it's trivia nights with friends, family board game evenings, or impromptu dance-offs, shared play activities offer opportunities for authentic connection and interaction, boosting interpersonal relationships significantly.

3.6. Stress Management and Playfulness

Moderate stress can indeed stimulate productivity, but chronic stress hampers our physical health and cognitive capacity. In an era where stress levels are soaring alarmingly, the role of playfulness as a stress coping mechanism is becoming increasingly apparent. A study by the American Psychological Association indicated that just above 50% of adults utilize hobbies to manage stress, hinting towards play's role as a mental stress-absorber.

3.7. Playfulness and Productivity

Playfulness and productivity needn't be on two opposite ends of a spectrum. An investment in momentary playfulness yields dividends in productivity. Our brain's concentration ability operates in natural cycles of intense focus interspersed with short breaks. Infusing these breaks with playful activities can help refresh the mind and reset concentration levels. Hence, incorporating small, playful activities into your work routine can boost efficiency, leading to higher productivity.

3.8. Cultivating a Playful Attitude

The journey of reintegrating playfulness into everyday life starts with a shift in mindset. It involves dismantling barriers that prevent adults from embracing playfulness, such as societal expectations, self-doubt, or fear of judgment. Start small by reintroducing what you loved doing as a child or explore new hobbies. The essence of cultivating this attitude it to give oneself 'Permission to Play'.

To wrap up our expedition into the world of playfulness, we remember the words of George Bernard Shaw, "We don't stop playing because we grow old; we grow old because we stop playing." By embracing playfulness, we invite happiness, health, and creativity into our lives, contributing to a vibrant, resilient, and enriched life. So, let us consciously pause and engage in the empowering practice of playfulness, opening avenues of unending joy and fulfillment. As we continue the journey of life, let's take along our playful heart and illuminate the world around us with its effervescent energy.

Chapter 4. Stress-Busting: How Play Alleviates Adult Anxieties

We are surrounded by a plethora of stressors, be it deadlines, work-life imbalance, financial pressures, or simply the overwhelming stimuli from modern life. As these adult anxieties pile up, they have severe implications on our psychological well-being, immune system, and overall life quality. Having a tangible approach to manage our anxieties plays a key role in staying healthy. Residing in the heart of this stress-management sphere is the concept of play. Initially perceived as a trivial or non-productive activity for adults, this perception couldn't be further than the truth.

4.1. The Science of Stress and Play

The human physiological response to stress involves the production of cortisol, a hormone contributing to feelings of anxiety and apprehension. Research shows that engaging in playful activities drastically reduces these stress-induced hormonal levels, providing a sense of tranquility and calmness that lasts well beyond the playtime. In a 2019 study by the American Journal of Play, adults who incorporated play activities into their routine reported lower stress levels, better mood, and improved adaptability to unforeseen situations.

4.2. Forms of Adult Play

Learning to reconnect with our playful self involves understanding the different forms of 'play' for adults. They can include creative arts, dance, sports, video games, board games, and even everyday living activities with a touch of playful imagination. For instance, turning your cooking regime into a mini experimental culinary show lends a playful aspect to an otherwise ordinary routine.

4.2.1. Indoor and Outdoor Play

Indoor games like charades, puzzles, or building blocks stimulate intellectual curiosity, foster teamwork and turn time spent indoors into a fun, engaging experience. Outdoor games connect us with nature, remind us of our childhood playground memories and provide benefits of physical activity alongside the positive influence of sunlight and fresh air.

4.2.2. Digital Play

With advancements in virtual reality and online gaming, digital play forms an integral part of adult recreation in the digital age. Appreciating the fantasy world of video games or sweeping enemies in virtual battlefields serves as excellent escapism from real-world anxieties and invites a realm of positive, trouble-free interactions.

4.3. The Power of Laughter

Laughter is often described as the best medicine, but perhaps it can also be labelled as pure, therapeutic play. It's a universally shared language that generates social bonds, fosters a shared sense of joy, and acts as a potent stress-buster. Regularly indulging in humor-filled games or comedy shows can go a long way in keeping stress and anxieties at bay.

4.4. Play and Social Connections

Incorporating play into social activities has the dual benefit of relieving stress and improving social ties. Organizing fun activities in your social circles, like hosting game nights, participating in group sports, or jointly attending a dance class can create memorable experiences and strengthen bonds while vibrantly reducing stress.

4.5. Nurturing Mindfulness through Play

By fundamentally being a 'present-moment' activity, play inevitably instills mindfulness, allowing participants to immerse fully in the experience, temporarily forget their anxieties, and enjoy the current moment. As you jam with your favorite tune or carefully place that last piece of jigsaw puzzle, you engage in mindful play, where all focus is drawn away from stress to the task on hand.

4.6. Play as a Form of Exercise

Play isn't restricted to sitting around a board-game or spending hours lost in a fantasy video game. Physical play like sports, dance, or unleashing your inner child on a trampoline, all foster bodily movement and act as an excellent stress-relieving exercise. Certainly, as the adage goes, a healthy body promotes a healthy mind!

4.7. Circumventing Adult Barriers to Play

Although the importance of play is well recognized, many adults find it challenging to embrace playfulness due to perceived societal norms, lack of time, or impeding self-doubt. It requires taking conscious steps to redefine these barriers, such as prioritizing play, incorporating fun elements into everyday tasks, and inviting a cultural shift towards appreciating the creativity and joy of play.

This exhaustive insight into play's role in managing adult anxieties underscores our need to allay the misconceptions of adult play. Indeed, it is neither frivolous nor counterproductive, but an essential tool promoting mental serenity, creativity, and an overall healthier life. So go ahead, indulge your playful self - your brain, body, and mind will thank you for it.

Chapter 5. From Recess to the Office: Injecting Play into Everyday Life

The morning alarm jolts you out of your slumber, patting away the tendrils of dreamy lethargy. A quick breakfast, a hurried review of what the day entails and the race against the clock begins. This scenario can sound cruelly familiar to many adults circling their busy lives. In this relentless rush, the concept of play, something instinctual and vital to our human nature becomes an overlooked aspect. Yet, a call to revive playfulness isn't a call to abandon our post. It's a suggestion to inject a spark of playful delight into the daily life that fiercely demands dedication and seriousness.

5.1. Why Bring Play to Work?

Work takes a substantial chunk of adult life and to believe its atmosphere should only hold sternness and seriousness is an outdated notion. Amid the stretch of tight deadlines and never-ending meetings, introducing elements of play can remarkably boost productivity and induce calmness.

Playful activities stimulate our brain, fostering creativity and innovation. Neuroscience consistently points to the importance of play in enhancing problem-solving capabilities, setting free the shackled imagination, and improving agility in decision-making processes. The act of playing jogs the cognitive abilities, making people more receptive to new ideas and solutions.

Moreover, play fosters social connections. The collaborative nature of many games and activities leads to improved team dynamics and cohesiveness. By encouraging a social lubricant as powerful as play, workplaces can create a more inclusive, supportive environment.

5.2. Practical Strategies to Inject Play

Now that we understand the importance of play at work, the next step is to explore how to inject this element into our work lives. It requires minor adjustments and a shift in perspective rather than a radical change.

Establish Playful Spaces: No, this doesn't mean converting the conference room into a playground. It involves creating spaces that promote casual interaction and spontaneous creativity. It could be a shared lunch space where employees come together to relax, or a small corner of the office dedicated to creative activities like doodling or puzzle-solving.

Promote Playful Activities: Encourage team-building exercises with an element of fun. Contests, quizzes, role-play scenarios, and mini-games that stimulate creative and strategic thinking can foster team spirit and unearth your colleagues' hidden talents.

Instil Playful Mindset: Cultivate a mindset that views challenges as opportunities for play. Rather than pressuring employees to come up with the "right" solutions, stimulate curiosity, experimentation, and the enjoyment of the problem-solving process itself.

Allow Flexibility: Foster an environment that allows breaks for relaxation and refreshment, which often breeds creativity. Encouraging employees to take brief breaks to engage in enjoyable activities can rejuvenate the mind, leading to increased productivity and well-being.

5.3. The Diverse Faces of Play

The notion of play at work might evoke images of table tennis matches and board games, but it's far wider and profound. Play can take many forms and it doesn't limit to physically engaging diversions.

Cognitive Play: Includes activities like brainstorming, problem-solving, strategic games that stimulate the brain. These activities can be incorporated into routine work life via team meetings, workshops, or training sessions.

Physical Play: Involve some forms of physical activity, such as stretching exercises, office sports events, or even short walks.

Creative Play: Entails activities that let individuals express imaginations like painting, writing poetry, or crafting. Even simple acts such as doodling during breaks can serve as creative play.

Social Play: The play that involves socializing and forming connections. It could include team outings, office parties, or even lunch breaks together.

5.4. Transforming Stress into Playfulness

Work is often associated with stress. The challenging situations, deadlines, workload can cause workers to feel overwhelmed. However, incorporating play can help in managing such stress. Approaching work challenges with a playful mindset, accepting them as a game or a puzzle to solve, can transform the stressful nature of work.

Not every challenge at work can be 'played' away, but savoring the small playful moments in the journey can have a profound impact in mitigating the stress. At the end of the day, it is not just about changing what we do but also transforming how we perceive what we do.

5.5. Conclusion

Injecting play into everyday life at work is not a frivolous idea. Rather, it's a revolutionary approach towards enhancing productivity and overall well-being. Embracing the child-like joy of play in our structured adult lives can make us happier, more creative, and more resilient, thus paving a path for a healthier work environment and a balanced life.

Chapter 6. Bonding Over Laughter: The Social Dynamics of Play

Laughter has its mysterious way of bonding people together. From a hearty chuckle with a friend over a shared memory to a room full of people laughing at a live comedy show, laughing together establishes a feeling of connection and community.

6.1. The Science Behind Bonding and Laughter

The physiological benefits of laughter are many - it reduces stress hormones, releases endorphins, and increases our pain tolerance. Laughter is also a social tool, with its essence lying at the heart of relationships. When we laugh with others, it is a communal activity that promotes group bonding and enhances our sense of social identity.

In his comprehensive study, Dr. Robert Provine, a neuroscientist and author of "Laughter: A Scientific Investigation," noted that 80% of our laughter isn't in response to any structured form of jokery. Instead, it occurs in daily social interactions, when we are with other people. This evidence suggests that the primary function of laughter may not be humor but social connection.

Adding to that, work from the Stanford University School of Medicine identified laughter instigating an endorphin surge through the activation of particular brain regions. Endorphins, often termed 'feel good' hormones, lead to feelings of happiness and even euphoria.

6.2. Play Leads to Laughter

Play begets laughter. But what does adult play look like? For children, play is typically centered around the exploration of their environment, role play, or games. For adults, play can be more cerebral and multifaceted. It may encompass more structured events such as board games, races, or team sports. Alternatively, it can be creative pursuits such as painting or acting. It might even be something less conventional: Adventure games, escape rooms, or a friendly mock debate.

The paramount element of adult play is that it's fun and enjoyable. When the mind is occupied with an engaging task that incites delight, a natural bi-product is laughter.

6.3. Shared Laughter as a Social Glue

The importance of shared laughter in strengthening relationships cannot be understated. Sharing a joke, a funny story, or an amusing experience builds a common emotional platform, reducing social differences and enhancing feelings of unanimity.

High-quality experimental studies from world-renowned institutes have underscored the role of shared laughter in bonding. A landmark research piece by Dunbar, Curry, Stamatakis, et al., published in the Journal of Human Nature, suggests that shared laughter releases endorphins across numerous brain regions that facilitate the establishment and maintenance of social bonds.

6.4. Laughter in the Workplace

In the workplace, laughter has a significant role to play. It's not just about interjecting fun into the daily grind. Instead, it strengthens teamwork, reduces stress, and fuels creativity.

Business scholars have studied humor and laughter at the workplace extensively, finding links to increased productivity and improved team cohesion. Andrea C. Morales, a professor in the marketing department at the W. P. Carey School of Business at Arizona State University, concluded that appropriately applied humor increases creativity by breaking conventional thinking patterns and paving way for innovative solutions.

6.5. Boosting Morale Through Laughter

Experts advocate for incorporating laughter-triggering activities into the professional environment as a part of keeping the workforce's morale high. Playfulness, often encouraged by elements of gamification, can foster a lighter atmosphere, significantly improving both work productivity and employee satisfaction.

6.6. Play and Laughter in a Digital World

As we navigate increasingly towards a digital world, play isn't left behind. From online multiplayer games playing with friends to hilarious memes shared across social networks, laughter and playfulness have found new platforms.

Hilarious GIFs, funny videos or humorous exchanges on social media platforms have all become a part of our digital interactions. Despite the lack of physical presence, shared laughter remains potent in building and nurturing relationships and communities online.

6.7. Concluding Notes

Reviving play in our lives and inviting more laughter isn't just about adding enjoyment or relieving stress. It's about celebrating the human existence and our incredible capacity to connect over simple, shared experiences. It's about transforming daily routines into moments of joy. If there's one piece of wisdom to take away, it's this: Sharing playful moments – and the laughter that accompanies them – fosters connections, binds communities, and brings more happiness into our lives. Play isn't a luxury – it's a necessity, no matter what age we might be.

Chapter 7. Boosting Creativity: The Link between Playfulness and Innovation

An intriguing canvas begins to reveal itself when we commence our exploration into the interconnected realms of playfulness and creativity. It is within this dynamic and vibrant interplay where adults can recapture their misspent youth's open-minded flexibility and curiosity, which instigates innovation.

7.1. The Nature of Playfulness and Creativity: A Primordial Connection

If you look closely enough, all forms of play emulate the energetic dance of the creative process: an initial spark of inspiration, an exciting exploration of potential, a period of development and refinement, and finally, a moment of realization. This inherent rhythm of playfulness harmonizes perfectly with our innate creative capacities.

Research conducted by Bateson & Martin (2013) affirms that playfulness in mammals, including humans, lays the foundation for creativity and problem-solving abilities. The play mindset fosters a relaxed environment conducive to divergent thinking, the genesis of creativity.

7.2. Exploring Psychological Underpinnings

Dr. Stuart Brown, a renowned psychiatrist, suggests that nurturing playful behaviors positively influences an individual's ability to generate diverse ways of understanding the world, ultimately boosting their creative capacities. During play, we deviate from the rigidity of regular tasks, venturing into a realm of 'what if'. This freedom allows for a psychological flexibility, providing the fertile ground in which the seeds of creativity can sprout.

Moreover, positive psychology sheds light on how playful states can enhance individuals' creative performance. The broaden-and-build theory by Fredrickson (2001) posits that positive emotions (stemming from playfulness) broaden a person's momentary thought-action repertoire, promoting innovative ideas and actions.

7.3. A Biopsychological View

From a biopsychological standpoint, the relation between playfulness and creativity gains even intriguing dimensions. During a state of playful engagement, neurochemical reactions, such as the release of endorphins, dopamine, and serotonin, foster joyful and relaxed feelings. These reactions are linked to a heightened state of creativity.

Nerve growth factors, especially in the hippocampus (a brain region crucial for learning, memory, and mood regulation), are also stimulated during play. This process nourishes our capacity for adaptability – a cornerstone of creative thinking.

7.4. Case Studies: From Silicon Valley to Scandinavian Schools

Observing how successful companies engage with playfulness illuminates the concept further. For instance, Google's policy of allowing employees to spend 20% of their time on personal projects – known as 'Innovation Time Off' – has resulted in successful ventures like Gmail and AdSense. This approach resonates with the playful exploration concept, spurring creativity and productivity simultaneously.

A similar approach is used in Scandinavian schools where 'play breaks' are embedded into the curriculum, the results of which have shown to increase students' creativity and problem-solving abilities.

7.5. Practical Ways to Boost Creativity through Play

1.Write a 'Dream Journal': Upon waking, write a brief description of your dreams. This practice embraces the playful, imaginative realm of the unconscious, nurturing innovative thinking.

2.Do something new every day: This can be as simple as trying a new food, exploring a new route to work, or learning a new language. Stepping out of your habitual patterns promotes mental agility.

3.Use 'Idea Boxes': Write down a variety of ideas, situation, or objects, and randomly draw to combine them. This is a playful way to engage divergent thinking and develop unexpected connections.

4.Set aside 'Creative Play Time': Commit to a period each day for undirected, exploratory, creative activities.

5.Perform Improvisation: Activities such as improvisational theatre exercises can help develop mental flexibility and spontaneity, cornerstones of creativity.

7.6. Conclusion: Playfulness – The Gateway to Innovation

This intricate dance between playfulness and creativity embraces the challenges of everyday adult life, inspiring solutions that were previously unimaginable. It is through this conscious return to the playful mind of our childhood that we can rekindle the inherent innovator within us. Thus, infusing playfulness into adulthood is not a mere reminiscing of childhood fantasies. Instead, it's an empowering tool that enhances our creative capacities, driving us towards a life marked by innovation, imagination, and constantly renewed perspectives.

Remember, in the words of George Bernard Shaw, "We don't stop playing because we grow old; we grow old because we stop playing." Therefore, keep that playful spirit alive and channel it creatively, the benefits would undoubtedly go beyond a simple laugh or a fleeting moment of joy. It might just well be the spark that leads to your 'eureka' moment.

Chapter 8. Overcoming Barriers: Shedding the Taboos Around Adult Play

The societal norms of adulthood often dictate a certain seriousness, which inadvertently pushes the joy and spontaneity of playfulness aside. However, relinquishing this essential human experience constitutes a significant loss, both socially and psychologically. This section will dissect the common barriers preventing adults from playing and offer practical advice on how to dismantle these walls.

8.1. Unlearning Societal Expectations

One of the toughest barriers to overcome when re-incorporating play into the adult realm is the societal pressure to 'act our age'. Adults are often expected to be responsible, professional, and composed at all times. This, in turn, shadows the freedom to indulge in play and exuberance.

To challenge these ingrained expectations, adults need to understand that playfulness does not equate to immaturity or irresponsibility. Scientifically, play stimulates neurochemical changes that promote stress relief, improve cognitive functionality and boost creativity, effectively aligning play with utmost productivity and effectiveness. Hence, replacing the term 'child's play' with 'human's play' can be a crucial cognitive shift in destigmatizing adult play.

8.2. Overcoming Fear of Judgment

The fear of judgment or embarrassment stands as another significant hurdle in championing the cause of adult play. Lighthearted behavior often deviates from the established image of a traditional adult, leading many to suppress playful characteristics in public scenarios.

Such fears can be mitigated by starting small and private. You could allocate time for private play- perhaps a dance session in the privacy of your room or a therapeutic painting session. Gradually introducing these playful practices into more public aspects of life can inure one to potential judgement and infuse play naturally into everyday routines.

8.3. Reevaluating the Perception of Time

With to-do lists stretching miles long and constant demands vying for attention, incorporating 'idle' playtime might seem indulgent, if not outright wasteful. However, this perspective stems from a misunderstanding of the role and impact of play in our lives.

Play is not idle time, but highly productive in promoting mental well-being, reducing stress, and enhancing social interactions. A quick game of charades or an impromptu dance-off can reenergize the brain, infuse positivity and increase output quality when one returns to work. Thus, shattering the perception of play as a time-waster forms an essential component of liberating adult play.

8.4. Shifting Away from Excessive Digitization

Digital technology has elevated interconnectedness and convenience to unparalleled heights. But, the resulting overdependence lays subtle traps, converting leisure time into yet more screen time - a phenomenon labeled as 'digital-only leisure'.

Disconnecting from digital mediums for play isn't easy, but is feasible. Begin by substituting some digital games with traditional board games or rediscovering the joy of outdoor sports. Instead of viewing videos, one could attend a live performance. Counteracting the digital overdose with hands-on, tactile experiences can reintroduce the thrive of physical play.

8.5. Reconnecting with the Joy of Play

For many, the memory of carefree play is buried deep under immediate adult concerns. Reconnecting with this forgotten joy requires conscious rediscovery.

Reflect on what kind of play resonated with you as a child. Was it the imaginative world of role-plays, the competitive spirit of sports, or the liberation of art and crafts? Ascertain what kindles your playfulness now – it could be the same as before or new activities altogether. This connection forms the basis of reaffirming play as a meaningful, joyful, and useful participant in adult life.

In conclusion, overcoming the taboos surrounding adult play may be a challenging endeavor. The journey will invariably involve confronting societal norms, fears of judgement, and personal inhibitions. But as we crawl, walk, then gallantly stride towards a more playful existence, the benefits reaped will illuminate the beauty of play, not just instinctive to children, but native to all humans. By embracing play, adults stand to gain a happier, more balanced and ultimately, a more fulfilling life.

Chapter 9. Play as Therapy: Case Studies of Success

The transformative power of play isn't just a concept plucked from thin air. It's backed by countless hours of research and myriad experiences. In this section, we delve into real-life examples of people employing play as a form of therapy, achieving fantastic results in improving mental health and overall life satisfaction.

9.1. The Case of John: Small Changes, Big Impact

John, a 35-year-old software engineer, lived a life revolving around his work. The pace of his job-induced stress and the constant need to stay ahead of the learning curve had turned him into a bundle of nerves. His therapist recommended introducing simple playful activities into his daily routine.

John began with playing a 15-minute online chess game during his lunch break. Despite initially dismissing it as frivolous, he found it a gratifying distraction from his work. Besides, the competitive aspect of the game fired up his adrenaline and learning strategy began to feel less like work and more like fun.

He further integrated play into his life by starting his mornings with a 10-minute doodling session. This exercise allowed him to express his emotions, feelings, or whims in a way that words could not. The colors began to relieve his stress and the fun of creating something without expectations lightened his mood.

After incorporating these playful activities, not only did John's stress level reduce significantly, but his efficiency and creativity at work also improved. The regular breaks improved his focus, and the infusion of fun left him feeling refreshed and recharged. His case clearly underlined the connection between productivity and playfulness—an approach that defies the conventional workspace mentality.

9.2. Sandra's Story: Play Enhancing Communication

Sandra, a middle-aged homemaker, faced difficulty in expressing her emotions. She felt isolated and found it challenging to connect with family members and friends. Her therapist recommended she incorporate game nights into her routine.

Every weekend, Sandra started inviting over a few friends and family for an evening of games. From classic board games like Scrabble and Monopoly to interactive party games like charades, these casual, friendly competitions became a medium for her to express herself.

Interestingly, Sandra discovered she could share laughter, joy, and even disappointment during these games, something she struggled with in her daily interactions. The playfulness loosened her inhibitions and gradually improved her communication skills.

Within a few months of regular game nights, Sandra not only felt more connected with her loved ones but also experienced a decrease in anxiety levels. The play had worked as a practical therapy for her, building bridges where none existed before.

9.3. Adam's Experience: Transformative Role-playing

Adam, a university professor, suffered from a lack of self-confidence, which hindered his lectures and student interactions. He sought help from a therapist, who recommended introducing role-playing into his daily routine.

Adam started experimenting with role-playing in safe and controlled environments, initially acting out different roles in front of the mirror. From a confident lecturer to a charismatic talk show host, he tried various roles, making a game out of it.

He gradually noticed a remarkable change. These playful exercises began to boost his confidence as he discovered different aspects of his personality. Playing a confident individual helped him feel more empowered in his actual role.

Adam's transformation was noticeable; his delivery improved in lectures and his interactions were more eloquent and assured. He found a unique way to communicate effectively with his students, and his overall performance as a lecturer improved.

Through these case studies, the role of playfulness as a form of therapy in nurturing well-being, managing stress, and improving communication can be appreciated. Importantly, playfulness should not be seen as a luxury or a waste of time. Instead, it's a necessity, a natural state of joy that we all need to reignite, cherish, and incorporate into our daily lives—no matter the age.

Chapter 10. Guided Games: Practical Approaches to Adult Playfulness

Playfulness is a vital aspect of human life. It is an innate disposition that enables us to approach activities with spontaneity, joy, and a sense of wonder. Unfortunately, as we transition into adulthood, we often relegate playfulness to the sidelines in favor of more 'serious' pursuits. Yet, many leading psychologists and life coaches argue that integrating play into our daily routines is actually a powerful strategy for enhancing our emotional, social, and cognitive well-being.

10.1. Reclaiming Play as Adults

As we navigate adulthood, we often suppress our playful impulses, finding them incompatible with our responsibilities. Obligations like work, household chores, and caring for children or elderly parents can leave little room for playful activities. Life becomes a series of tasks to complete rather than experiences to savour. However, psychologists insist this doesn't have to be the case. Instead, we can choose to infuse elements of play and playfulness into our routines, reinvigorating our lives with creativity and joy.

Adult playfulness should not be misunderstood as childishness. It involves purely adult skills like improvisation, mindfulness, problem-solving, humor, and perspective-taking. In the realm of play, we can exercise these skills in a relaxed setting, often finding new and unexpected connections or solutions.

10.2. Games as Vehicles of Play

Games represent one of the most recognizable and accessible forms of play. Whether board games, role-playing games, sport activities or video games, these structured pursuits offer a myriad of benefits. They stimulate our imaginations, foster social connections, encourage shared laughter, and provide a sense of achievement. Most importantly, they act as natural stress-relievers, helping us unwind and mentally switch off from pressing concerns.

10.3. Creating a Game Plan

Incorporating games into our routines might seem challenging initially. However, with some creativity, flexibility, and perseverance, we can find numerous avenues. You might start by scheduling a game night with friends, joining a local sports club, or setting aside time for a solo video gaming session. Whatever type of game resonates with you, the crucial factor is to engage in an activity you find joyful and relaxing.

10.4. Embracing Solo Play

Not all games require other players. Many engaging solitary games, including puzzles, brainteasers, and digital games, can be pursued individually. These activities can stimulate the mind, fostering concentration, pattern-recognition, and problem-solving skills. Moreover, solo games often provide a calm refuge in stressful times, giving you space to reconnect with your inner world.

10.5. Facilitating Social Connection Through Games

Games can also be a social conduit, facilitating connection and camaraderie among friends, families, and even strangers. They become a shared experience, defined by cooperation, competition, and fun. In these dynamic environments, we can practice important social skills like negotiation, empathy, and effective communication.

10.6. Virtual Games: Gateway to a Digital Playground

In the age of technology, digital games offer another platform to foster playfulness. Video games, online trivia, even virtual reality, can not only entertain but also stimulate cognitive development and emotional resilience. However, it's crucial to maintain a balance, ensuring digital gaming doesn't interfere with physical exercise or face-to-face social interactions.

10.7. The Therapeutic Power of Role-Playing Games

Role-playing games (RPGs), often associated with fantasy worlds and adventuring quests, have profound therapeutic potential. By stepping into different characters and navigating unfamiliar narratives, players can explore their own strengths, weaknesses, and emotions in a safe, imaginative context. This process allows players to confront personal challenges, learn empathy, and experiment with various solutions or responses.

10.8. Balancing Play and Responsibility

While games and playfulness offer numerous benefits, it's essential to strike a balance with life's responsibilities. A healthy play-life balance ensures that we have time for both nurturing our playful side and attending to necessary duties.

In conclusion, reintroducing playfulness in adulthood through games has the potential to boost our mental health, decrease stress, facilitate social connections, and cultivate cognitive skills. Our everyday routines can transform from monotonous tasks to vibrant experiences interspersed with joyful moments of play. As the art of play gets revived, we might just rediscover the joy and vivacity we remembered from childhood but had forgotten that, as adults, we could also embrace.

Remember, the purpose of games and play is enjoyment and relaxation, so choose activities that make you feel alive, recharged, and connected with your essence. As they say, 'All work and no play makes Jack a dull boy', never forget that playfulness is not age-dependent; it's a mindset that can transform any activity into an experience full of joy, creativity, and enthusiasm.

Chapter 11. Stepping into the Future: The Evolution of Play for Enhanced Well-being

The landscape of human experience has long been punctuated by play. From the earliest prehistoric paintings to the contemporary digital age, humans have engaged in shared activities for enjoyment, escape, and expression. As we traverse into the future, let us take a moment to cast an introspective gaze into the evolution of play and the role it is destined to serve in shaping our mental well-being.

11.1. The Play in Prehistory

The first humans interacted with their environment through a playful lens, being naturally drawn towards exploration and experimentation. Children would mimic adults, engaging in pseudo hunting, berry picking, shelter building, and other essential survival activities that we now define as play. Evolutionary psychologists suggest that such behavior was not merely about fun but was vital for the development of skills that ensured survival and reproduction.

11.2. Moving to Agricultural and Industrial Eras

The advent of agriculture shifted humans from nomadic hunter-gatherers to settled farmers. More structure was imposed on the act of play, becoming a tool for instilling societal norms and values primarily through story-telling, ritual dances, and games. With the Industrial revolution, play was increasingly seen as an unnecessary luxury or as an activity solely for children, thereby resulting in a widening gap between work and play.

11.3. Post-Industrial Age and the Rise of Structured Leisure

In the post-industrial age, technology has compartmentalized our time and life into highly structured fragments- work, sleep, leisure, inducing an artificial barrier between seriousness and playfulness. Leisure time became more organized around specific activities such as sports, hobbies, or entertainment media. Work and play were polarized, weakening the intrinsic connection between enjoyment and productivity.

11.4. The Digital Age: Play and Technology

In recent decades, technological advancements have reshaped the nature of play. Video games, social media, and digital simulations provide diverse opportunities for creativity, collaboration, and mental stimulation. However, the ubiquity of technology and its potential to isolate individuals raises questions around the quality and authenticity of digital play. It's crucial to strike a balance between engaging in solitary digital play and maintaining social connections that bolster mental health.

11.5. Futuristic Visions: Play for Wellness

As we set our eyes on the future, experts urge us to reconfigure our understanding of play, to see it as a lifelong necessity rather than a childhood pastime. Future trends in play therapy, gamification of work and education, and emphasis on play-based wellness interventions are all steps towards retrieving the essence of playfulness, eroding the artificial barrier between work and play, and enshrining play as a fundamental, natural aspect of human life, crucial to mental health and overall well-being.

11.6. Play Therapy: Healing through Play

Play therapy has proven effective in treating children with psychological issues, and now its principles are being applied to adults. Adulthood challenges like anxiety, depression, or relationship struggles can be addressed through play-based therapeutic interventions that foster expression, self-discovery, and emotional healing.

11.7. Gamification: Combining Work and Play

Gamification is revolutionizing the workplace and education sectors by integrating game elements into a non-game context to enhance motivation, engagement, and productivity. The vision is clear - make work feel more like play to reap the cognitive rewards of playfulness.

11.8. Play-Based Interventions for Wellness

Play-based interventions are increasingly emphasized in wellness programs. Immersive recreational activities, passion-driven hobbies, playful mindfulness exercises, and creative performance arts can all promote relaxation, psychological resilience, and mental vitality.

11.9. Embracing Playfulness: A Journey towards Wholeness

To make playfulness an integral part of future lifestyles, a holistic shift in societal attitudes is required. Schools, workplaces, and homes must all champion the cause of adult playfulness. We must foster environments that encourage creativity, innovation, and freedom to explore without judgment or fear of failure.

A promising future awaits wherein play is not a luxury but a need; not a distraction but a contributor to productivity; not a symbol of irresponsibility but an emblem of balanced living. Play has indeed evolved over centuries from an instinctive survival tool to a structured cultural practice and then to a corrective therapeutic aid. Now, we are called upon to initiate the next phase - to view play as an integral element of our mental well-being and a key performer in our journey towards wholeness.

While we may not know the form play will take in years to come, the certainty of play's significance remains unflinching. Despite numerous shifts and a few misconceptions, the play of the past sets a strong stage for a playful future. The challenge lies in imbuing our daily routines with playfulness, reigniting the sparks of creativity and joy.

Looking ahead, we can envision a society where mental health is fostered through a balanced cohabitation of work and play. Together, we could redefine the essence of a playful life, recognize its integral role in personal development, and ensure that healthy mental well-being is not just a wishful dream but a palpable reality. And that is the future of play - a future that sounds invigorating, fulfilling, humanizing, and, above all, fun.

Printed in Great Britain
by Amazon